HOW TO CURE ANXIETY

JACK FOWLER

TABLE OF CONTENTS

INTRODUCTION

Anxiety is an emotional, physiological state that occurs when we carry on apprehensively (stress that something terrible or destructive may happen). Apprehensive behaviors have effect on the body, and a body that turns out to be excessively stressed can get to be symptomatic. That is indications on the grounds that acting excessively uncertainly is the primary wellspring of the anxiety that causes the body to show symptoms.

The individuals who assert that anxiety isn't destructive don't comprehend the situation at the disorder level. Of course, mild uneasiness is innocuous; but when it gets to the disorder level it can bring about great hardship and lifestyle disability.

If you are encountering problematic anxiety, I urge you to effectively address it with the goal that it doesn't adversely influence your wellbeing. Tending to your dangerous anxiety can help you come back to ordinary and enduring health.

Series of good self-improvement information and personal therapy, counseling, and coaching is the best approach to overcome anxiety.

Anxiety Disorders are as predominant as Depression. It is evaluated that 1 in 9 individuals in Ireland will encounter an anxiety issue in their lifetime. 1 in 10 individuals counsel their GP with indications of anxiety, most not knowing that they are anxiety symptoms. Uneasiness issue can happen at any age. Numerous have an onset in youth or childhood. Some begin in adulthood.

Anxiety issue may happen because of hereditary predisposition or encounters in life (early encounters or late encounters). In spite of the fact that we may depict anxiety that is felt generally, most anxiety issues fit into a particular anxiety disorder.

ANXIETY DISORDERS ARE:

PHOBIAS: an unreasonable apprehension of an item, circumstance or place that prompts avoidance. The four primary groupings of phobias are: Blood injury fear, Agoraphobia, Specific phobia, and Social fear.

PANIC DISORDER: this includes serious anxiety connected with an error of physical indications where a man supposes they will die or 'go mad'.

GENERALIZED ANXIETY ISSUE: includes a component of "worry" which gets out of control for the individual. They will worry over a wide range of aspects of their life and will likewise have 'stresses over the worry'.

OBSESSIVE COMPULSIVE DISORDER: includes cycles where obsessive considerations are results to anxiety and afterward compulsions take place to decrease that uneasiness. There are 4 primary subtypes of Obsessive Compulsive Disorder: symmetry obsessions, sexual obsessions, harm to others and contamination.

BODY DYSMORPHIC DISORDER: includes great distress because of imaginations that prompts behavioral change.

HEALTH ANXIETY: includes intemperate uneasiness about wellbeing which includes considerations about having an ailment and dying which prompts behavioral changes.

POST-TRAUMATIC STRESS DISORDER: includes extreme apprehension and anxiety which identifies with the experience of traumas. There are particular manifestations present, for example, flashbacks, and upsetting thoughts of the traumas, nightmares and avoidance.

HABIT DISORDERS: are presentations of practices which are repeated such as hair pulling, nail biting, skin picking.

SEXUAL DIFFICULTIES: includes challenges in sexual relationships. For men these troubles include premature ejaculation or low libido, erectile dysfunction. For ladies the challenges are anorgasmia, vaginismus.

Many of the above mentioned Anxiety Disorders can be treated. Cognitive Behavioral Psychotherapy is a confirm Therapy that studies has been discovered successful in treating the above anxiety issue. There are particular Cognitive Behavioral Psychotherapy treatment models to treat each of the anxiety issue above.

In this book, we are going to have better understanding of anxiety and the best ways to deal with the situation.

Happy reading!

CHAPTER 1

WHO SUFFERS FROM ANXIETY?

Anxiety is a condition which definitely impacts everybody sooner or later for the duration of their lives. We have numerous unpleasant circumstances through life; work weights, school, college, family, accomplices, social commitments/responsibilities, and so on which can regularly leave us with sentiments of nervousness inferable from the anxieties and conflicts of life.

Mild Anxiety in itself is not generally destructive and can help in making a man more ready and concentrated on any prompt dangers and/or challenges, which is clearly valuable. Be that as it may, when this nervousness gets to be constant or turns out to be an excessive amount it gets to be undesirable and can impact typical everyday life.

Sadly, why sentiments of nervousness and anxiety itself are frequently covered by the sufferer is a far reaching issue, and is regularly endured peacefully. All things considered it is not amazing to find that numerous individuals that experience the ill effects of anxiety including someone you could never suspect (e.g. Barbara Streisand, Kim Basinger,) and they won't discuss it or concede they have been languishing over quite a while in silence.

In the United States it is evaluated 18.1% of the adult populace suffer from anxiety or frenzy issue. It is additionally twice as normal in females as it is in men. Also numerous cases start in youth with the normal period of onset being 11 years old!

Anxiety Disorders are the most widely recognized emotional wellness issue alongside depression, influencing the number of inhabitants in Ireland and Europe. They represent a comparative level of anxiety and incapacity in society as cancer or coronary illness.

There are no precise figures to proof the commonness of Anxiety Disorders in Ireland. It is evaluated that 1 in 9 people will experience essential nervousness issue over their lifetime. Just a small amount of these people get fitting treatment which is an extraordinary step as it has been confirmed reliably that with therapy the most of sufferers can accomplish an enduring change.

Anxiety issue has nothing to do with a specific age. The time of onset is very variable going from childhood and adolescence to adulthood.

Frequently anxiety issues are connected with other anxiety disorder, for instance agoraphobia consolidated with panic issue. There is additionally the relationship between anxiety issue and different issues, for example, substance/alcohol misuse and depression.

Anybody can be a victim of anxiety regardless of the status or type. It has no respect for whoever you may be, your money, political or religious status.

FEATURES OF ANXIETY DISORDER

- Altered physical sensations – sickness, palpitations.
- Altered contemplations - worry, irrational thinking
- Altered conduct - avoidance, restless
- Altered feelings - panic, fear

In this way, take heart! Try not to give anybody a chance to let you know that you need to "live with" an anxiety issue for whatever is left of your life.

Of course, the situation can get tough, yet it gets to be harder the more you hold up, put things off, and give into it. I have seen such a variety of people who overcome anxiety issue, and that is why i can't agree that anxiety is something that must be surrendered to, acknowledged as it may be, or persevered until the end of time.

Research has demonstrated that individuals who take an interest in dynamic, organized psychological behavioral treatment are not just better after treatment is over...but they keep on feeling better over the long haul. Basically, life just improves and better and better.

CHAPTER 2

WHAT IS ANXIETY?

Anxiety refers to sentiments of nervousness, stress, or feelings of fear, commonly around a forthcoming occasion where the result is dubious, or where the individual feels he or she won't be up to the task. Anxiety is ordinarily experienced in pressured circumstances, for instance, preceding making a speech or sitting an exam. Sentiments of anxiety can likewise emerge following an upsetting occasion, similar to a mishap where the individual is left feeling shaken. Anxious emotions are typically connected by physical sensations, for example, a racing heart, churning stomach, and light headedness.

Anxiety is more than simply feeling pushed or stressed. While stress and anxious sentiments are typical reactions to a circumstance where we feel pressure, they generally come to an end once the distressing circumstance has passed, or "stressor" is evacuated.

Anxiety is the point at which these anxious sentiments don't die down – when they're continuous and exist with no specific reason or cause. It's a genuine condition that makes it difficult to adapt to day by day life. Everybody feels restless now and again; however for somebody encountering anxiety, these emotions can't be effectively controlled.

Anxiety is the most widely recognized psychological wellness condition in Australia. Generally, one in four individuals – one in five men and one in three ladies – will encounter anxiety at some phase in their life. In a 12-month time frame, more than two million Australians experience anxiety. The sooner individuals with anxiety get help, the more probable they are to recoup.

For those adults who experience the anxiety symptoms, regular life can be somewhat more difficult than we can figure out. There's the shocking trepidation of specific occasions, the approaching thought about a fit of anxiety and steady physical manifestations — and it can be all the more troublesome when you feel like nobody else comprehends what's going on.

There are stigmas that society has made for anxiety sufferers, however much more chances to overcome them. From sensitive expressions to extraordinary fears, there are some things individuals with anxiety know to be true and what everybody can do to offer assistance.

It's a typical day. You're prepared to take off the entryway when all of a sudden, chest constricts. Before long you're overwhelmed by trepidation — it's practically horrifying. What's more, there's nothing you can do to stop it.

Some panic appear unexpectedly, without a whisper of a notice, while others are apprehension prompted, brought on by standing up to the circumstance that gives them anxiety in any case. Notwithstanding when it happens (or how the experience influences you personally), it's rarely convenient — it's never pleasant. When somebody experiences one of these disorders, it's totally debilitating.

Anxiety doesn't simply torment the brain — physical indications can likewise originate from the confusion. A 2007 New Zealand investigation of members with excited digestive tracts proposes there's a connection between anxiety issue and the advancement of Irritable Bowel Syndrome. The large amounts of anxiety generally connected with tension can likewise create indications that range from hives and rashes to dry mouth and dizziness.

If you're experiencing anxiety, your fears are increased to a compelling degree — and it's something that doesn't as a matter of course leave. Getting on a plane or strolling into a room loaded with outsiders can get to be horrifying, and there isn't a speedy fix for how you're feeling.

In any case, the individuals who experience the indications of anxiety issue experience fear on a more profound level. We as a whole affair anxiety in some capacity, it helps us get ready for talking in public and it rouses us to hone or practice; everybody can identify with what that experience resemble.

It's a toxic cycle where your considerations turn into your stresses and your stresses turn into your contemplations. However, as indicated by one study distributed in the journal PLOS One; Analysts found that ruminating on negative contemplations is one of the greatest indicators of dejection and anxiety and the mental reaction to occasion's incident is significantly more fundamental than what really happened. Looking for help if anxiety sufferers begin to get excessively lost in the negative thoughts can offer assistance to overcome the situation. Those feelings the sufferers feel are genuine. They're not simply made up in their mind.

There is completely an approach to proceed onward in case you're experiencing anxiety, whether it's through talk therapies, drug, or both. There are different techniques for treatment — it's about finding what works best for you. There are approaches to get help and there is more than one alternative accessible. Anxiety sufferers can get over it. There's no reason that you ought to endure in the way that you're suffering.

CHAPTER 3

WHAT CAUSES ANXIETY?

Anxiety disorder can have various distinctive causes. Some individuals are inclined to anxiety issue because of their hereditary makeup. Others basically can't deal with anxiety well. At times, you may have a anxiety issue without encountering any of these causes.

Everybody gets anxious, frazzled, and restless — yet if you're continually encountering nervousness and don't generally know why, you could have an anxiety disorder.

Specialists make a diagnosis of generalize anxiety issue when patients have anxiety indications, (for example, frequent headaches, <u>insomnia</u>, difficult in concentrating, and constant worry) for over six months, without justifiable reason. In any case, what causes the anxiety-ridden to fuss over daily occasions — circumstances that people basically forget about? Analysts don't totally see all the causes; however they do realize that anxiety is connected to various astonishing triggers, from weight reduction supplements to thyroid issues.

Anxiety issue might be brought about by substance abuse, brain chemistry, genetics, medical factors, environmental factors, or a combination of these. It is most usually activated by the anxiety in our lives.

Anxiety is a reaction to outside strengths, however it is conceivable that we make ourselves anxious with "negative self-talk" - a propensity for always letting yourself know the most exceedingly awful will happen.

ANY OF THE BELOW OFFENDERS MAY CAUSE ANXIETY

Psychological Health and Family history

Some individuals who experience anxiety conditions may have a hereditary inclination towards anxiety and these conditions can some of the time keep running in a family. However, having a guardian or close relative experience anxiety or other psychological wellness condition doesn't mean you'll consequently develop anxiety. Various different components assume a part, including current life circumstances, adverse life experiences and personality factors.

Personality factors

Research proposes that individuals with certain personality characteristics will probably have anxiety. For instance, kids who lack self-esteem, inhibited, timid, easily flustered, perfectionists or need to control everything, sometimes show anxiety indication during adults, childhood or as adolescence.

Stressful occasions

Anxiety conditions may show up as a result of one or more distressing life occasions. Normal triggers include:

- Employment change or Work Stress
- Change in living courses of action
- Giving birth and Pregnancy
- Relationship issues or Family
- Emotional shock following traumatic occasion
- Physical or Emotional abuse, trauma, sexual or verbal
- Family member, loss of a friend or Death

Physical wellbeing issues

Chronic physical diseases can likewise results to anxiety conditions or effect on the treatment of either the anxiety or the physical ailment itself. Basic chronic conditions results to anxiety conditions include:

- coronary illness and Hypertension
- Diabetes
- Asthma

Some physical conditions can lead to anxiety conditions, similar to an overactive thyroid. It can be helpful to see a specialist and be evaluated to figure out if there might be a medicinal reason for your sentiments of anxiety.

Other emotional well-being conditions

While some individuals may encounter a tension condition all alone, others may encounter various anxiety conditions, or other psychological well-being conditions. Anxiety and Depression conditions regularly happen together. It's imperative to check for and get help for all these conditions in the meantime.

Substance use

Some individuals who experience anxiety may utilize liquor or different medications to help them deal with their condition. In many cases, this may prompt individuals building up a substance use problem alongside their anxiety condition. Liquor and substance use can bother anxiety conditions especially as the impacts of the substance wear off. It's vital to check for and get help for any substance use conditions in the meantime.

Everybody's distinctive and it's regularly a blend of factors that can add to building up an anxiety condition. Remember that you can't generally recognize the reason for anxiety or change troublesome circumstances. The most critical thing is to perceive the signs and manifestations and look for support and guidance.

Types of Anxiety

Numerous individuals with anxiety experience manifestations of more than one types of anxiety issue, and may encounter despondency also. It's critical to look for guidance early in case you're encountering uneasiness. Your symptoms may not leave all alone and if left untreated, they can begin to take once again your life.

THERE ARE NUMEROUS TYPES OF ANXIETY. THE SIX MOST COMMON ANXIETY ISSUES ARE:

Generalized Anxiety Disorder (GAD): A man feels restless on most days, stressing over heaps of various things, for a time of six months or more

Social fear (Social phobia): People has an extreme trepidation of being condemned, humiliated or embarrassed, even in regular circumstances, for example, talking openly, eating in the public, being emphatic at work or making casual conversation.

Particular phobia: A you feels exceptionally dreadful around a specific item or circumstance and may put forth an admirable attempt to dodge it, for instance, travelling on a plane or having an injection. There are various sorts of fears.

Obsessive compulsive disorder (OCD): People have progressing intrusive musings and fears that bring about anxiety. In spite of the fact that the individual may recognize these thoughts as senseless, they frequently attempt to calm their nervousness via completing certain practices. For instance, an apprehension of contamination and germs can prompt steady washing of hands and garments.

Post-traumatic stress disorder (PTSD): This can happen after a man encounters a traumatic incident (e.g. disaster, accident, assault, war). Indications can incorporate trouble relaxing, disquieting dreams or flashbacks of the occasion, and shirking of anything identified with the occasion. PTSD is analyzed when a man has side effects for no less than a month.

Agoraphobia: Agoraphobia is the trepidation of going out in the public, either open spaces or the trepidation of being in new places. Numerous individuals with agoraphobia either never leave their home, or do anything they can to abstain from traveling to anyplace other than their home and office. Some individuals can go to the market or other well known spots, yet generally encounter extreme fears anyplace else.

Numerous people that have agoraphobia additionally have *panic disorder.* That is because for some people, agoraphobia is frequently caused by panic attacks. Individuals experience panic attacks in the public places, so they begin to keep away from request to maintain a strategic distance from panic attacks until they are reluctant to go outside. Many people experience agoraphobia after traumatic incidents too.

Agoraphobia is common among adult. Many people likewise fear losing control (both mentally and physically), making them dodge social circumstances. Not everybody living with agoraphobia invests all their energy in their home. Indeed, a portion of the symptoms of agoraphobia include:

- Obsessive apprehension of associating with people
- Severe anxiety or uneasiness at whatever point you're in a situation other than the home or any environment where you're not in control.
- Feelings of pressure notwithstanding amid consistent exercises, for example, chatting with outsiders, or even simply venturing outside.
- Preoccupation with how to secure yourself or discover wellbeing if some kind of inconvenience happens, even with little motivation to assume that trouble will happen.
- Finding that your own particular fears are keeping you from going out and living because of fears.

Numerous people experience moments where they feel helpless outside and like to stay safe in their homes. In any case, when the trepidation appears to endure for longer time, or is keeping you away from carrying on with an agreeable life, you may have agoraphobia.

Panic disorder

Many people have panic attacks, which are extreme, overpowering and frequently wild sentiments of tension consolidated with a scope of physical manifestations. Somebody having a panic disorder may encounter excessive perspiration, dizziness, chest pain and breath. Some of the time, individuals encountering a panic disorder think they are showing at least a bit of heart attack or are going to bite the dust. If someone has intermittent panic attack or steadily panic for over a month, they're said to have panic disorder.

CHAPTER 4

HOW TO BATTLE BACK

Anxiety can put obstacle to your day by day life and disturb your prosperity. If you are feeling restless right now, then you might be uncomfortable and startled. To stop your nervousness, there are loads of things that you can do at this moment that will help you to feel better. To lessen the odds of future anxiety, you can join some self improvement practices and roll out way of life improvements. You may likewise need to look for the assistance of an advisor if anxiety is disturbing with your day by day life.

Practice deep breathing: Profound deep breathing is a standout amongst the best approaches to rapidly lessen anxiety. You can do profound breathing in anyplace and it just takes a couple of minutes to feel the effects.

- To do profound breathing, sit down in an agreeable position.
- Place your hands over your stomach, just beneath your ribcage.

- Take deep long breath and count to five. Focus on maneuvering the air into your chest and abdomen
- Then, hold the breath for a few moments and breathe out gradually.
- Keep breathing out and breathing in gradually for around 5 - 10 minutes.

Attempt dynamic muscle relaxing: Muscle relaxing is additionally a fast approach to diminish anxiety. Muscle relaxing is the point at which you strained and discharge the muscles in your body each one in turn, moving from the tips of your toes to the highest point of your head.

- Begin by setting down somewhere agreeable.
- Close your eyes and after that curl your toes under in order to tighten the muscles in your toes.
- Then, discharge the tension in your toes
- Strained your feet by flexing them.
- Then, discharge this strain then, move to your calves.
- Continue to strained and discharge the muscles in your body one by one until you get to your forehead.

Call a companion: Associating with somebody and communicating how you feel may likewise calm anxiety. Try calling a companion to discuss what is at the forefront of your thoughts. On the other hand get together with a companion and talk through your emotions in person.

Avoid imparting how you feel by means of social media or blog, attempt to associate with somebody face to face or on the telephone. Video talk is another alternative in the event that you can't leave your home or work environment.

Physical activity: Any kind of physical movement can be calming. Activity is even viewed as a successful approach to treat anxiety, so if you are feeling restless, activity is an extraordinary option. You can do anything that you appreciate, however attempt to do 20 - 30 minutes of activity consistently.

- **Attend a yoga class:** Yoga gives incredible reinforcing and extending practices alongside profound breathing and reflection systems that can diminish your uneasiness.

- **Dance around in your room:** You don't have to go outside to get some exercise. Have a go at putting on some of your most loved music and moving around in your room.

- **Go for a walk:** Strolling is most likely the least demanding approach to get some snappy physical movement. Try taking a walk around your neighborhood.

Imagine a serene scene: Envisioning a quieting spot may likewise help you to quiet down rapidly. Try envisioning a most loved place, including what it would seem like, smells, sounds and feels. Stay in this peaceful space for whatever length of time that you like.

For instance, you may envision that you are sitting in a wonderful place in the summer. ...seeing delightful wildflowers surrounding you, notice the fragrance of the flowers and grass, hear the sound of a tender breeze blowing, and feel the sun glow on your skin.

Try to be busy: Distraction can help you to feel less anxious too. Attempt to drive yourself to accomplish something that will hold your consideration when you are feeling restless. In the wake of taking part in an action for 20 to 30 minutes, your anxiety may leave.

For example, you could get a book and begin reading, organize your desk, play with your dog or cat, or take a relaxing bubble bath.

Lavender scented lotion: Lavender has been appeared to be powerful at decreasing anxiety in a few circumstances, for example, before taking a test. Consider wearing a lavender scented cream or keeping a container of lavender oil nearby so you can smell it from time to time. Other oils may likewise give anxiety diminishing results, for example, bergamot, lemon, clary sage, and Roman chamomile,

Music: Listening to music may likewise lessen your anxiety. Music treatment has even been observed to be powerful for patients why waiting for surgery. Try listening to some alleviating music, for example, Jazz, classical, or simply listen to something that you appreciate.

Make inquiries to challenge your anxious sentiments. Make a rundown of target inquiries you can ask yourself to challenge your explanations for your anxiety. By taking time to rationalize your nervousness, you may feel like it has less control over you. Some inquiries you may ask yourself include:

- What proof is there to support that something is truly wrong?
- What proof is there to support that the circumstance is really not as terrible as it shows up?
- What are the chances that the direst outcome imaginable can really happen?
- What are the more probable results?
- How would I advice a companion who had this anxiety or one like it?

Plan a time for your anxiety: Since you will undoubtedly feel anxious once in a while, you may think that it's accommodating to plan some daily stress time. This will help you as far as possible on your anxiety, as opposed to permitting yourself to feel restless throughout the day.

- Schedule a range of 20 to 30 minutes every day to stress and feel anxious. In a perfect world, it ought to be the same time every day and your stressing ought to be done in the same spot.
- If anxieties show up outside of your stress period, write those nerves down. Advise yourself that you will have sufficient time to stress over it later.
- Reflect on your anxieties amid your stress period. You may even find that some of your anxieties have vanished

when you are prepared to stress over them.

Put your feelings in paper: Distinguishing your emotions and putting them on paper may likewise help you to feel better. When you are feeling anxious, take a seat and simply write on how you feel. You may even need to begin a contemplations diary to monitor the majority of your anxious musings. One approach to compose your entries in a thoughts diary is to divide what you compose into three columns.

- The first section can be something like: What is going on? On the other hand, what is the circumstance? In this section, you can portray where you are, what you are doing, who you are with, and so on.
- The second segment can be something like: What am I considering? In this area, you can write on the anxious musings that you are having.
- The third section can be something like: How anxious am I? For this segment, you can simply compose a number from 1 to 10 to speak to how anxious you feel.

Advise yourself that the way you feel is not permanent: Infrequently when you feel anxious, you may feel like it is changeless and stress that you will never feel great again. This can be entirely frightening, so you may need to advise yourself that your emotions are just temporary. Try saying something like: "This is just a little moment in time." Or, "These emotions won't last."

Divert your contemplations to the present: Thinking about the past or future can incite anxiety, so preparing yourself to concentrate on the present can likewise be a decent approach to lessen anxiety. Concentrating on the present can likewise make it less demanding for you to manage the issues or assignments that are facing you right now.

To make yourself more mindful of the present minute, pay consideration on what is going on around you. What do you see? Who is there? What do you feel? What do you smell? You might need to practice meditation to end up more focused around the present. Meditation is additionally an awesome approach to decrease anxiety.

CHAPTER 5

GETTING HELP

If your anxiety is meddling with your everyday life, then it may be a smart thought to look for the assistance of a psychological health professional, for example, a therapist or counselor. Talk treatment is a powerful approach to diminish uneasiness and to learn compelling tools for taking care of anxiety-inciting circumstances.

For instance, you might need to look for treatment if you have been pulling back from your loved ones, staying away from certain spots out of apprehension, or experiencing considerable difficulties on work or school in view of your anxiety.

ATTEMPT COGNITIVE TREATMENT: Cognitive therapy concentrates on changing your contemplations and practices with a specific aim to lessen your uneasiness. By experiencing cognitive treatment with an authorized psychological health professional, you recognize, challenge, and supplant the negative contemplations that make you feel anxiety.

For instance, you may find that you frequently ponder internally, "I am going to die," and this mussing may make you feel restless. With cognitive behavioral treatment, you will figure out how to recognize this idea as it happens and change the thoughts into something positive, for example, "I am going to be a blessing to my generation."

Cognitive treatment is something that you ought to just experience with an authorized therapist. Get some information about utilizing psychological treatment as a component of your treatment arrangement.

CONSIDER EXPOSURE THERAPY: The Exposure therapy helps you to confront the fears that make you feel restless. After some time, you may face your fears for more timeframes or build the force of your exposure. Subsequently, your anxiety and fear levels ought to improve.

For instance, if you are afraid of flying, then you may start by envisioning that you are in a plane. After some time, you may work up to air terminal, taking a short flight, and after that, as a last objective, taking a cross-country or abroad flight.

You ought to just experience exposure treatment with the direction of an authorized therapist. If your fears cause you to feel uneasiness, then converse with your specialist about including some exposure treatment into your treatment program.

GET SOME INFORMATION ABOUT MEDICATIONS: There are a few diverse sorts of prescription accessible for anxiety, which you might need to consider if you experience difficulty controlling your nervousness by different means. Remember that you will need to see a therapist (a restorative specialist who works in psychiatry) to acquire drugs for anxiety. A few meds you may consider include:

ANTIDEPRESSANTS: A few antidepressants can diminish anxiety, yet these take around four to six weeks to begin working. Some basic antidepressants that can help with anxiety incorporate Celexa (citalopram), Zoloft (sertraline), Prozac (fluoxetine), Paxil (paroxetine), and Lexapro (escitalopram).

BUSPIRONE: This medication is a mild sedative that takes around two weeks to start working. It is like benzodiazepines; however it is much milder and it doesn't have much side effects. Buspirone is likewise less inclined to be addictive.

BENZODIAZEPINES: These are the most widely recognized anxiety medications. They work quickly to lessen tension, yet they can be addictive. It is best to utilize these drugs for serious anxiety as it were. A few benzodiazepines incorporate Ativan (lorazepam) Xanax (alprazolam), Klonopin (clonazepam), and Valium (diazepam).

BETA BLOCKERS: Some high blood pressure drugs known as beta blockers can likewise help with the physical manifestations of anxiety. These are considered off-label physician recommended drugs since beta blockers are endorsed for heart issues and hypertension. Some beta blockers incorporate Inderal (propranolol) and Tenormin (atenolol).

CHAPTER 6

STEPS YOU CAN TAKE TO HELP SOMEONE WITH ANXIETY DISORDER

Attending to someone with anxiety issue can be frustrating. Regularly, those people will delay getting treatment for reasons identified with their ailment. Help is accessible, however, and it frequently is as easy as knowing where to swing to get to it. One of the initial steps you can bring to help somebody with anxiety issue is to contact somebody who has knowledge of what they've been experiencing and have the capacity to place the person in contact with the expert resources you'll need for your loved one.

Conversing with Someone with Anxiety Disorder

It's never simple conversing with somebody with anxiety issue about the problem you think you find in their life. The person may get hostile or defensive; translating what you say as an entirely pointless personal assault against him/her. And that is a sign that they didn't know they had anxiety disorder.

Sending a letter to someone who has anxiety disorder can in some cases useful as it takes away a significant part of the confrontational element and permits the subject to think about your worries without feeling any need to mount a defense against you.

Another conceivable approach to attempt to break the defense of the person with anxiety disorder and adequately approach him is to gather loved ones and family for intervention. Anxiety issue aren't entirely addictions, but since a considerable lot of the same protection components will regularly become an integral factor to oppose treatment, once in a while comparative ways to deal with existence of an issue can be fruitful.

Where to Find Anxiety Treatment for a Friend or Family Member

One of the difficulties to effective treatment is failure to detect the issue at earliest point, and knowing where to get anxiety treatment for a companion or relative. It's absolutely the rare individuals who have broad information of the resources and treatment alternatives that exist to those who experience the ill effects of anxiety disorder.

This is the reason, most importantly, it is crucial to quickly perceive the signs that a friend or family member may be battling with anxiety and act accordingly. Finding the fitting resources can be troublesome and tedious, which is the reason it can be such an alleviation to know caring professionals are accessible at any times of the day and night to accept your call and interface with you to help you deal with this disabling disorder.

Watching over somebody with anxiety or depression can be challenging. However, each individual experience is one of a kind; there are parts of the role that are regular to numerous carers.

Things you can do to help somebody with anxiety or depression are:

- Discourage the individual from utilizing unapproved medications or liquor to feel better.
- Encourage loved ones to welcome the anxiety sufferer and stay in contact; however, don't pressure to partake in any activities.
- Encourage and advice the person to confront their fears with support from psychologist.
- Let the individual know whether you've seen an adjustment in their conduct.
- Spend time conversing with the person about their encounters and let them realize that you're there to listen without being judgmental.
- Assist the person to discover information about anxiety and depression from a library or website.
- Encourage the individual to attempt to get enough rest,

eat sound nourishment and do exercise.

- Suggest the individual see a health professional and/or help them to make an arrangement.
- Agree to go with the person to the health professional.

It is unhelpful to:

- Mount pressure on them by instructing them to 'start thinking responsibly.
- Stay away or maintain a strategic distance from them
- Tell them they simply need to get out more or stay busy

Pressure them to mingle with people more or wipe out how they're feeling with medications and liquor.

CONCLUSION

Thanks for reading this book; I hope you've learnt about anxiety and how to deal with the situation. Anxiety can be the causes of other health issues. Don't waste much time if you've been suspecting that someone in your surrounding is experiencing anxiety disorder. Be your brother's keeper today by approaching the person with proper manner and assisting him/her to get treatment for anxiety disorder. If you are the one suffering from anxiety, you can recoup by following all what I discussed in this book but you have to visit a licensed expert in order to get proper treatment.

Take the first step today by stepping out of your door to seek help. You are not the only one in this situation; there are millions of people in the world undergoing the same problem. Don't allow discouragement or fear to hinder you of getting necessary treatment, and your life will bounce back to normal.

Thanks for the time taking to read this book. Hope you enjoy it!

www.ingramcontent.com/pod-product-compliance
Lightning Source LLC
Chambersburg PA
CBHW061931280526
45787CB00004B/1561